# Jokes

## OVER 500 OF THE FUNNIEST JOKES THAT CHILDREN WILL LOVE

*M. PREFONTAINE*

Published by MP Publishing

Copyright © 2016

**Q: What did one toilet say to the other?**

*A: You look a bit flushed.*

**Q: What do you get when you cross a dinosaur with fireworks?**

*A: Dino-mite*

**Q: What do you call an old snowman?**

*A: Water*

**Q: Why do bicycles fall over?**

*A: Because they are two-tired*

**Q: Why do dragons sleep during the day?**

*A: So they can fight knights*

**Q: Were you long in the hospital?**

*A: No, I was the same size I am now*

**Q: What is a frog's favorite exercise?**

*A: Jumping Jacks*

**Q: Why couldn't the pirate play cards?**

*A: Because he was sitting on the deck*

**Q: What happened to the naughty little witch at school?**

*A: She was ex-spelled*

**Q: Why was the belt arrested?**

*A: Because it held up some pants*

**Q: How do all the oceans say hello to each other?**

A: They wave

**Q: Why don't blind people like to sky dive?**

A: Because it scares their guide dog

**Q: What do you call a bear with no teeth?**

A: A gummy bear!

**Q: What do you call cheese that isn't yours?**

A: Nacho cheese

**What do you call a dinosaur with one leg?**

A: Eileen

**Q: Where do cows go for entertainment?**

A: To the moo-vies

**Q: How do you know if there's an elephant under your bed?**

A: Your head hits the ceiling

**Q: Why are elephants so wrinkled?**

A: Because they take too long to iron

**Q: Who hides in the bakery at Christmas?**

A: A mince spy

**Q: How do you keep an elephant from charging?**

A: Take away her credit card

**Q: Why did the elephant paint himself different colors?**

A: So he could hide in the crayon box

**Q: How can you tell if an elephant has been in your refrigerator?**

A: By the footprints in the butter

**Q: What is the difference between elephants and grapes?**

A: Grapes are purple.

**Q: What two letters of the alphabet do snowmen prefer?**

A: I.C.

**Q: What do you call a cow with no legs?**

A: Ground beef

**Q: What do you call a cow with two legs?**

A: Lean meat

**Q: What do you call a pig that knows karate?**

A: A pork chop

**Q: What does a duck like to eat with soup?**

A: Quackers

**Q: Why are ghosts bad liars?**

A: Because you can see right through them

Q: What animal needs to wear a wig?

A: *A bald eagle*

Q: What do you call a fly without wings?

A: *A walk*

Q: What do you call an alligator in a vest?

A: *An investigator*

Q: What has four wheels and flies?

A: *A garbage truck*

Q: Why did the man run around his bed?

A: *Because he was trying to catch up on his sleep*

Q: Why did the math book look so sad?

A: *Because it had so many problems*

Q: Can a kangaroo jump higher than the Empire State Building?

A: *Of course! The Empire State Building can't jump*

Q: Why did the chicken cross the playground?

A: *To get to the other slide.*

Q: Why do bees have sticky hair?

A: *Because they use honeycombs*

Q: Why was the man running around his bed?

A: *He wanted to catch up on his sleep.*

Q: **Why is 6 afraid of 7?**

A: *Because 7 8 9*


Q: **What's black and white, black and white, black and white?**

A: *A penguin rolling down a hill*


Q: **Why do cows wear bells?**

A: *Because their horns don't work*


Q: **What does a snail say when it's riding on a turtle's back?**

A: *Weeeee*


Q: **What happens when a frog parks in a no-parking space?**

A: *It gets toad away*


Q: **How did the barber win the race?**

A: *He knew a short cut.*


Q: **Did you hear about the pregnant bed-bug?**

A: *She's having her babies in the spring.*


Q: **Which is the best athlete to have with you on a cold day?**

A: *A long jumper.*


Q: **Did you hear about the two men arrested for stealing batteries and fireworks?**

A: *One was charged but the other was let off.*

**Q: What do you get if you eat Christmas decorations?**

A: Tinselitus

**Q: Why did the jelly baby go to school?**

A: Because he really wanted to be a smartie.

**Q: What bug is welcome in apartments?**

A: Ten-ants.

**Q: Where do ants eat?**

A: At a restaur-ant.

**Q: What is the biggest ant in the world?**

A: An eleph-ant.

**Q: Why don't oysters share their pearls?**

A: Because they're shellfish

**Q: What's even bigger than that?**

A: A gi-ant

**Q: What does an octopus wear in the winter?**

A: A coat of arms.

**Q: What bird is always out of breath?**

A: A puffin.

**Q: What do porcupines say after they kiss?**

A: Ouch

Q: What does a cat like to eat on a hot summer's day?

A: A mice cream cone.

Q: What do you call a great dog detective?

A: Sherlock Bones

Q: Where do you find a dog with no legs?

A: Right where you left him.

Q: What kind of animal is always found at baseball games?

A: The bat.

Q: How do you make a skunk stop smelling?

A: Pinch its nose closed.

Q: Where is the best place to park a dog?

A: In a barking lot.

Q: How does a snowman lose weight?

A: He waits for the weather to get warmer

Q: Why do Hummingbirds hum?

A: They've never learned the words

Q: Which are the strongest creatures in the ocean?

A: Mussels.

Q: What do you call Rodents that play Hockey?

A: Rink Rats

**Q: What do you get when you cross a Bear and Skunk?**

A: Winnie the Pehew

**Q: What do you get if you cross a chili pepper, a shovel and a terrier?**

A: A hot-diggity-dog

**Q: What animal needs oil?**

A: The mouse, because it squeaks.

**Q: Why can't a leopard hide?**

A: Because he's always Spotted.

**Q: What's the biggest moth in the world?**

A Mam-moth.

**Q: Why did the lion spit out the clown?**

A: Because he tasted funny.

**Q: What is the best way to communicate with a fish?**

A: Drop it a line

**Q: What is a mosquito's favorite sport?**

A: Skin-diving.

**Q: Why couldn't the chicken find her eggs?**

A: She mislaid them.

Q: What jam can't be eaten on toast?

A: *A traffic jam*


Q: Why are chefs hard to like?

A: *Because they beat eggs, whip cream, and mash potatoes*


Q: Where do burgers like to dance?

A: *At a Meatball*


Q: What kind of food is crazy about money?

A: *A dough-nut*


Q: What did 'Ronald McDonald' give 'Wendy' for their engagement?

A: *He gave her and Onion Ring*


Q: Which bean do kids like best?

A: *The Jellybean.*


Q: Why did the man go into the pizza business?

A: *He wanted to make some dough.*


Q: Why do toadstools grow so close together?

A: *They don't need Mushroom.*


Q: What's the last thing you take off, before you go to bed?

A: *Your feet off the floor*

**Q: What has four wheels and flies?**

*A: A garbage truck*

**Q: Why won't a bicycle stand up when it's not moving?**

*A: It's too tired.*

**Q: What did the beach say as the tide came in?**

*A: Long time, no sea.*

**Q: Who can shave six times a day, and still have a full beard?**

*A: A barber.*

**Q: How do you get a Pikachu on a bus?**

*A: You Pokemon*

**Q: Why does Peter Pan always fly?**

*A: Because he can 'Neverland'.*

**Q: What do you call a piece of wood with nothing to do?**

*A: Bored*

**Q: Why did the gardener plant his money?**

*A: He wanted the soil to be rich.*

**Q: What did one angel say to the other angel?**

*A: Halo.*

**Q: What did Cinderella say when her photos weren't ready?**

*A: Someday my prints will come.*

Q: Why did the man put his money in the freezer?

A: *He wanted cold hard cash*

Q: What did the porcupine say to the cactus?

A: *Is that you mommy?*

Q: What do you get when you cross a snowman with a vampire?

A: *Frostbite.*

Q: How do crazy people go through the forest?

A: *They take the psycho path.*

Q: What do you get from a pampered cow?

A: *Spoiled milk.*

Q: Where do polar bears vote?

A: *The North Poll*

Q: What sickness do horses hate the most?

A: *Hay fever*

Q: What did Geronimo say when he jumped out of the airplane?

A: *Me.*

Q: Where do snowmen keep their money?

A: *In snow banks.*

Q: What's brown and sticky?

A: *A stick.*

**Q: Why do sea-gulls fly over the sea?**

A: Because if they flew over the bay they would be bagels

**Q: What dog keeps the best time?**

A: A watch dog.

**Q: Why did the tomato turn red?**

A: It saw the salad dressing

**Q: What did the grape do when it got stepped on?**

A: It let out a little wine

**Q: Where do bees go to the bathroom?**

A. At the BP station

**Q: What did the judge say when the skunk walked in the court room?**

A. Odor in the court.

**Q: What do you call a horse that lives next door?**

A: A neigh-bor

**Q: What did the water say to the boat?**

A: Nothing, it just waved.

**Q: What did the fish say when he swam into the wall?**

A: Dam

Q: Why don't skeletons fight each other?

A: *They don't have the guts.*


Q: How do dinosaurs pay their bills?

A: *With Tyrannosaurus checks.*


Q: What do you call a dinosaur that smashes everything in its path?

A: *Tyrannosaurus wrecks.*


Q: How do you make an egg laugh?

A: *Tell it a yolk.*


Q: Did you hear the joke about the broken egg?

A: *Yes, it cracked me up*


Q: How do you prevent a Summer cold?

A: *Catch it in the Winter*


Q: How does a pig go to hospital?

A: *In a hambulance.*


Q: If a long dress is evening wear, what is a suit of armor?

A: *Silverware.*


Q: What bird can lift the most?

A: *A crane.*

Q: What bone will a dog never eat?

A: A trombone.


Q: What clothes does a house wear?

A: Address.


Q: What country makes you shiver?

A: Chile.


Q: What did one elevator say to the other?

A: I think I'm coming down with something


Q: What did one magnet say to the other?

A: I find you very attractive.


Q: Why was the baby ant confused?

A: Because all of his uncles were ants


Q: What did Tennessee?

A: The same thing Arkansas.


Q: What did Delaware?

A: Her New Jersey.


Q: What did the mother broom say to the baby broom?

A: It's time to go to sweep.


Q: What did the necktie say to the hat?

A: You go on ahead. I'll hang around for a while.

Q: What did the rug say to the floor?

A: *Don't move, I've got you covered.*


Q: What do bees do with their honey?

A: *They cell it.*


Q: Why was Cinderella thrown off the basketball team?

A: *She ran away from the ball.*


Q: Why were the teacher's eyes crossed?

A: *She couldn't control her pupils.*


Q: What do you call a song sung in an automobile?

A: *A cartoon.*


Q: Why does a flamingo stand on one leg?

A: *Because if he lifted that leg off the ground he would fall down*


Q: What do you get if you cross a chicken with a cement mixer?

A: *A brick layer*


Q: What do you get if you cross an insect with the Easter rabbit?

A: *Bugs Bunny.*


Q: What happens when frogs park illegally?

A: *They get toad.*


Q: What has 6 eyes but can't see?

A: *3 blind mice.*

**Q: What has one horn and gives milk?**

A: A milk truck.

**Q: What is a tree's favorite drink?**

A: Root beer.

**Q: What is the best thing to do if you find a gorilla in your bed?**

A: Sleep somewhere else.

**Q: What kind of cats like to go bowling?**

A: Alley cats.

**Q: What kind of eggs does a wicked chicken lay?**

A: Deviled eggs.

**Q: What lies on its back, with one hundred feet in the air?**

A: A dead centipede.

**Q: What do you call a country where everyone has to drive a red car?**

A: A red carnation.

**Q: What would the country be called if everyone in it lived in their cars?**

A: An in-car-nation.

**Q: What's gray, eats fish, and lives in Washington, D.C.?**

A: The Presidential Seal.

**Q: What's green and loud?**

A: A froghorn.

**Q: What's round and bad-tempered?**

A: A vicious circle.

**Q: Where did the farmer take the pigs on Saturday afternoon?**

A: He took them to a pignic.

**Q: Where do fortune tellers dance?**

A: At the crystal ball.

**Q: Why did the doughnut shop close?**

A: The owner got tired of the hole business

**Q: What did the asparagus say to the mushroom?**

A: You're a fun guy.

**Q: What's the best thing to put into a pie?**

A: Your teeth.

**Q: What did the nut say when it got a cold?**

A: Cashew.

**Q: What is it called when a cat wins a dog show?**

A: A cat-has-trophy.

**Q: What do you get if you cross a fish and an elephant?**

A: Swimming trunks.

**Q: What do you call a sleeping bull?**

A: A bulldozer.

**Q: What do you call a sheep with no head or legs?**

A: A cloud.

**Q: What season is it when you go on a trampoline?**

A: Springtime.

**Q: What does a cloud wear under its raincoat?**

A: Thunderwear.

**Q: What did the tornado say to the other tornado?**

A: Let's twist again like we did last summer.

**Q: What happens if it rains cats and dogs?**

A: You need to watch for poodles.

**Q: What is Tarzan's favorite Christmas carol?**

A: Jungle Bells.

**Q: What do snowmen like to do after Christmas?**

A: Chill out.

**Q: What did the cat have for breakfast?**

A: Mice Crispies

**Q: What did the cow say on December 25th?**

A: Mooey Christmas

Q: Why didn't the turkey have any Christmas dinner?

A: *Because he was stuffed.*


Q: What did the snowman say to the other snowman?

A: *Can you smell carrots?*


Q: What sneaks around the kitchen on Christmas Eve?

A: *Mince spies.*


Q: How do you make a tissue dance?

A: *You put a little boogie in it.*


Q: Why can't you hear a pterodactyl in the bathroom?

A: *Because it has a silent pee.*


Q: What does a nosey pepper do?

A: *Gets jalapeno business*


Q: What do you call a deer with no eyes?

A: *No eye deer.*


Q: What do you call a deer with no eyes and no legs?

A: *Still no eye deer.*


Q: The past, present and future walk into a bar.

A: *It was tense.*


Q: What goes "ha ha thump"?

A: *A man laughing his head off.*

**Q: Why are pirates so mean?**

A: I don't know, they just arrrrrrrrr.


**Q: Why was Tigger looking in the toilet?**

A: He was looking for Pooh.


**Q: What do you get when you throw a piano down a mine shaft?**

A: A flat miner.


**Q: What do you get when you put a candle in a suit of armor?**

A: A knight light.


**Q: What do you call a sleepwalking nun?**

A: A roamin' Catholic.


**Q: How do you make holy water?**

A: You boil the hell out of it.


**Q: What did the 0 say to the 8?**

A: Nice belt


**Q: Why did the orange stop?**

A: Because, it ran outta juice.


**Q: What's brown and sounds like a bell?**

A: Dung


**Q: Why did the stop light turn red?**

A: You would too if you had to change in the middle if the street

Q: What did the green grape say to the purple grape?

A: *Breathe*

Q: If you're American in the living room, what are you in the bathroom?

A: *European*

Q: Is it raining cats and dogs?

A: *It's okay, as long as it doesn't rein-deer*

Q: What does the man in the moon do when his hair gets too long?

A: *Eclipse it*

Q: What did the cat say when he lost all his money?

A: *I'm paw*

Q: What's a ghost's favorite fruit?

A: *Boo-berries.*

Q: Why did the robber take a shower?

A: *Because he wanted to make a clean getaway.*

Q: What do you call a shoe made from a banana?

A: *A slipper.*

Q: What did the apple tree say to the farmer?

A: *Stop picking on me!*

**Q: Why are there fences around cemeteries?**

*A: Because people are dying to get in.*

**Q: Why did the pony get detention?**

*A: Because he was horsing around.*

**Q: Why did the teacher have to wear sunglasses?**

*A: Because her students were so bright.*

**Q: Which bus crossed the ocean?**

*A: Columbus.*

**Q: What do you call a fish with no eye?**

*A: A fsh.*

**Q: What does a cat on the beach have in common with Christmas?**

*A: Sandy claws*

**Q: What do gymnasts, acrobats, and bananas all have in common?**

*A: They can all do splits.*

**Q: What's a frog's favorite game?**

*A: Hopscotch.*

**Q: What day of the week does the potato look forward to the least?**

*A: Fry-day.*

**Q: What is Dracula's favorite fruit?**

A: Neck-tarines.

**Q: What does a skeleton order for dinner?**

A: Spare ribs.

**Q: What's a ghost's favorite dessert?**

A: Ice Scream.

**Q: How do monsters tell their fortunes?**

A: They read their horror-scopes.

**Q: Where does the witch park her vehicle?**

A: In the broom closet.

**Q: What do you call a witch who likes the beach but is scared of the water?**

A: A chicken sandwitch

**Q: What is a witch's favorite subject in school?**

A: Spelling.

**Q: Why couldn't the ghost see his parents?**

A: Because they were trans-parents.

**Q: What do you do if you're a fan of Dracula's?**

A: You join his fang club.

Q: Where do ghosts go for a swim?

A: *The Dead Sea.*


Q: Whom did the monster ask to kiss his boo-boos after he fell?

A: *His mummy.*


Q: What makes a skeleton laugh?

A: *When something tickles his funny bone.*


Q: What would you get if you crossed a teacher with a vampire?

A: *Lots of blood tests.*


Q: Why did the skeleton cross the road?

A: *To get to the body shop.*


Q: What do witches order at hotels?

A: *Broom service.*


Q: Why did the Cyclops stop teaching?

A: *Because he only had one pupil.*


Q: Why didn't Dracula have any friends?

A: *Because he was a pain in the neck.*


Q: Where did the witch have to go when she misbehaved?

A: *To her broom.*


Q: What's a ghost's favorite room in the house?

A: *The living room.*

**Q: What do birds do on Halloween?**

*A: They go trick or tweeting.*

**Q: Which monster is the best dance partner?**

*A: The Boogie Man.*

**Q: Why was the turkey arrested?**

*A: It was suspected of fowl play.*

**Q: What smells the best at Thanksgiving?**

*A: Your nose.*

**Q: Which side of the turkey has the most feathers?**

*A: The outside.*

**Q: Are turkey leftovers good for your health?**

*A: Not if you're the turkey.*

**Q: What do elves learn in school?**

*A: The elf-abet.*

**Q: What do you get if you cross a pine tree with an apple?**

*A: A pine-apple.*

**Q: What type of diet did the snowman go on?**

*A: The Meltdown Diet.*

**Q: What did the snowman have for breakfast?**

*A: Frosted Flakes.*

**Q: Why did the boy keep his trumpet in the freezer?**

A: Because he liked cool music.

**Q: What is Santa's dog called?**

A: Santa Paws

**Q: What's brown and sneaks around the kitchen?**

A: Mince spies.

**Q: What happened to the man who stole a calendar from the store?**

A: He got 12 months.

**Q: Why was Santa's helper sad?**

A: Because he had low elf-esteem.

**Q: What does Santa clean his sleigh with?**

A: Comet.

**Q: What did the stamp say to the envelope?**

A: I'm stuck on you.

**Q: What did the paper clip say to the magnet?**

A: I find you very attractive.

**Q: What kind of flower do you never want to get on Valentine's Day?**

A: Cauliflower.

**Q: What do elephants say to one another on Valentine's Day?**

*A: I love you a ton.*

**Q: Why is the forest so noisy?**

*A: Because the trees bark.*

**Q: What did the squirrel give for Valentine's Day?**

*A: Forget-me-nuts.*

**Q: What do you call two birds in love?**

*A: Tweet-hearts.*

**Q: What did the monster ask his sweetheart?**

*A: Will you be my Valen-slime?*

**Q: What did the farmer give his wife for Valentine's Day?**

*A: Hogs and kisses.*

**Q: What did the owl say to his sweetheart?**

*A: Owl be yours.*

**Q: What did the calculator say to the other calculator on Valentine's Day?**

*A: Let me count the ways I love you.*

**Q: What did one piece of string say to the other piece of string?**

*A: Will you be my Valen-twine?*

Q: Why did the boy bring a ladder to school?

A: *He wanted to go to high school.*

Q: What are there a lot of when turkeys play baseball?

A: *Fowl balls.*

Q: Where do pencils go for vacation?

A: *Pencil-vania.*

Q: What did the snowman order at Wendy's

A: *A Frosty.*

Q: Why can't skeletons play music?

A: *Because they have no organs.*

Q: How do you catch an unusual rabbit?

A: *Unique up on it.*

Q: What's the best way to talk to a T-Rex?

A: *From a distance.*

Q: What kind of music do mummies like best?

A: *Wrap.*

Q: Where can you learn to make ice cream?

A: *At Sundae School.*

Q: Why did the boy run around his bed?

A: *He was trying to catch up on his sleep.*

**Q: What do you call an elephant in a phone booth?**

*A: Stuck*

**Q: Which flower talks the most?**

*A: Tulips, because they have two lips.*

**Q: What did the spoon say to the knife?**

*A: You're so sharp*

**Q: How did the hairdresser win the race?**

*A: She knew a shortcut.*

**Q: Why are fish so smart?**

*A: Because they are always in a school.*

**Q: What did the dinner plate say to the cup?**

*A: Dinner's on me tonight.*

**Q: What did the triangle say to the circle?**

*A: I don't see your point.*

**Q: What's a rabbit's favorite kind of music?**

*A: Hip-hop.*

**Q: Where's a wall's favorite place to meet his friends?**

*A: At the corner.*

**Q: Where did the king keep his army?**

*A: In his sleeve.*

Q: Where do books hide when they're scared?

A: *Under their covers.*

Q: What's a scarecrow's favorite fruit?

A: *Strawberries.*

Q: Why can't the elephant use the computer?

A: *Because he's afraid of the mouse.*

Q: What do ghosts use to wash their hair?

A: *Sham-BOO.*

Q: What did the hamburger name her daughter?

A: *Patty.*

Q: Why do cowboys ride horses?

A: *Because they're too heavy to carry.*

Q: What is a math teacher's favorite type of dessert?

A: *Pi.*

Q: Why was the cafeteria clock always behind?

A: *Because it went back for seconds.*

Q: Why is 1+1=3 like your left foot?

A: *It's not right.*

Q: Where do kids in New York City learn multiplication?

A: *In Times Square.*

**Q: Why did Dracula's mother give him cough medicine?**

*A: Because he was having a coffin fit.*


**Q: What did Dr. Frankenstein get when he put a goldfish brain in the body of his dog?**

*A: Don't know, but it is great at chasing submarines.*


**Q: Why wasn't there any food left after the monster party?'**

*A: Because everyone was a goblin.*


**Q: Why did the vampire's lunch give him heartburn?**

*A: It was a stake sandwich.*


**Q: Dracula decided he needed a dog, which breed did he choose?**

*A: A bloodhound.*


**Q: What would you call the ghost of a door-to-door salesman?**

*A. A dead ringer.*


**Q: Who was the most famous French skeleton?**

*A: Napoleon bone-apart.*


**Q: Who won the skeleton beauty contest?**

*A: No body.*


**Q: What is a vampire's favorite holiday?**

*A: Fangsgiving.*

Q: What do skeletons say before they begin dining?

A: *Bone appetite*

Q: What is a ghoul's favorite drink?

A: *Slime juice*

Q: What do fishermen say on Halloween?

A: *'Trick-or-trout'*

Q: Where do spooks go to post a parcel?

A: *The ghost office.*

Q: What did the vampire say to the Invisible Man?

A: *'Long time, no see'*

Q: What did the mother ghost say her children?

A: *Don't spook until you're spooken to.*

Q: Why do witches wear name tags?

A: *So that they can tell which is witch*

Q: What do you call a witch who lives at the beach?

A: *A sand-witch.*

Q: What is a cat's favorite song?

A: *Three Blind Mice*

Q: Why don't angry witches ride their brooms?

A: *They're afraid of flying off the handle.*

**Q: What do witches put on their hair?**

A: *Scare spray.*

**Q: When is it bad luck to meet a black cat?**

A: *When you're a mouse.*

**Q: What happened when a boy vampire met a girl vampire?**

A: *It was love at first bite*

**Q: How does a girl vampire flirt?**

A: *She bats her eyes.*

**Q: What do you call a skeleton who won't work?**

A: *Lazy bones.*

**Q: What's a skeleton's favorite musical instrument?**

A: *A trom-bone*

**Q: Where do baby ghosts go during the day?**

A: *Dayscare centres.*

**Q: Why don't skeletons like parties?**

A: *They have no body to dance with.*

**Q: Who delivers presents to baby sharks at Christmas?**

A: *Santa Jaws*

**Q: What was the favorite game at the ghosts' birthday party?**

A: *Hide and shriek.*

**Q: Is it true that a lion won't attack if you hold a tree branch?**

A: *That depends on how fast you carry it*

**Q: What's the nickname for someone who put her right hand in the mouth of a lion?**

A: *Lefty*

**Q: Why do mummies make good employees?**

A: *They get all wrapped up in their work.*

**Q: Who did the ghost invite to his party?**

A: *Anyone he could dig up*

**Q: Who did Frankenstein take to the prom?**

A: *His ghoul friend.*

**Q: Why did the game warden arrest the ghost?**

A: *He didn't have a haunting license.*

**Q: How can you tell if a vampire likes baseball?**

A: *The night that he goes into a bat.*

**Q: Where do spooks water ski?**

A: *On Lake Erie.*

**Q: What kind of streets do zombies like to haunt?**

A: *Dead end streets.*

**Q: What has webbed feet, feathers, fangs and goes quack-quack?**

A: Count duckula.

**Q: What's a monster's favorite Shakespeare play?**

A: Romeo and ghouliet.

**Q: Who does Dracula get mail from?**

A: His fang club.

**Q: Why couldn't the astronaut book a room on the moon?**

A: Because it was full.

**Q: How do astronauts serve dinner?**

A: On flying saucers.

**Q: What's worse than raining cats and dogs?**

A: Hailing taxi's

**Q: How do you make an artichoke?**

A: Strangle it

**Q: What's the fastest vegetable?**

A: A runner bean.

**Q: What do you call two rows of vegetables?**

A: A dual cabbage way.

**Q: Why did the banana go to the doctor?**

A: *Because it wasn't peeling well.*

**Q: What did the apple skin say to the apple?**

A: *I've got you covered*

**Q: Why did the Tomato go out with a prune?**

A: *Because he couldn't find a date*

**Q: What did the lettuce say to the celery?**

A: *Quit stalking me.*

**Q: What is the different between a piano and a fish?**

A: *You can't tuna fish*

**Q: What do fish call a submarine?**

A: *A can of people.*

**Q: What did the father tomato say to the baby tomato whilst on a family walk?**

A: *Ketchup.*

**Q: What do you call a retired vegetable?**

A: *A has-bean.*

**Q: What do you call an angry pea?**

A: *Grump-pea.*

**Q: Why did the spider go on the internet?**

A: To make a Webpage.

**Q: What illness do martial artists get?**

A: Kung - Flu.

**Q: How do frogs send messages?**

A: Morse toad.

**Q: What's black and white and red all over?**

A: A newspaper.

**Q: What's red and green & wears boxing gloves?**

A: A fruit punch

**Q: What is the most romantic fruit salad?**

A: A date with a peach.

**Q: What do you get when you cross a potato with an onion?**

A: A potato with watery eyes.

**Q: Where were potatoes first fried?**

A: In Greece

**Q: What did the baby corn say to the Mum corn?**

A: Where's Popcorn

**Q: Where do baby apes sleep?**

A: In apricots

**Q: What game do elephants love to play?**

*A: Squash*

**Q: Why do fish live in salt water?**

*A: Because pepper makes them sneeze*

**Q: Where do mice park their boats?**

*A: At the hickory dickory dock.*

**Q: Where did the sheep go on vacation?**

*A: The baaaahamas.*

**Q: What do you call a cow that eats your grass?**

*A: A lawn moo-er.*

**Q: What is black, white and red all over?**

*A: A sunburnt penguin.*

**Q: How does a mouse feel after it takes a shower?**

*A: Squeaky clean.*

**Q: What do you call a cow in a tornado?**

*A: A milkshake.*

**Q: How do you catch a squirrel?**

*A: Climb up a tree and act like a nut*

**Q: What do you call a guy who lays in front of a door?**

*A: Matt*

**Q: Did you hear about the magic tractor?**

A: *It turned into the field.*

**Q: How do you keep someone in suspense?**

A: *I will tell you later.*

**Q: Why did the Queen go to the dentist?**

A: *To get crowns on her teeth.*

**Q: What do you call someone afraid of picnics?**

A: *A basket case*

**Q: What do you have if your dog can't bark?**

A: *Hush puppy.*

**Q: What's a snake's favorite school subject?**

A: *Hiss-tory*

**Q: What kind of dinosaur can you ride in a rodeo?**

A: *A Bronco-saurus*

**Q: What do you get if you cross a kitten and a fish?**

A: *A purr-anha.*

**Q: What's a whale's favorite game?**

A: *Swallow the leader.*

**Q: Why are horses so negative?**

A: *They always say 'neigh' to everything.*

**Q: What is the smartest animal in the whole world?**

A: A snake, as one can pull its leg.

**Q: Why is it easy to play tricks on lollypops?**

A: Because they're suckers.

**Q: Why did the cat get detention at school?**

A: Because he was a cheetah.

**Q: What happens when a cat eats a lemon?**

A: You get a sourpuss

**Q: Wat's a bats motto?**

A: Hang in there.

**Q: Why did the horse keep falling over?**

A: It just wasn't stable.

**Q: Why was the elf crying?**

A: He stubbed his mistle-toe.

**Q: What did the mummy rope say to the baby rope?**

A: Don't be knotty.

**Q: What did the big chimney say to the little chimney?**

A: You're too young to smoke.

**Q: What do you call a monster who's a genius?**

A: Frank-Einstein

**Q: Where do you find a chicken with no legs?**

A: *Exactly where you left it*

**Q: Which side of a chicken has the most feathers?**

A: *The outside*

**Q: What does a triceratops sit on?**

A: *Its tricera-bottom*

**Q: What do you call a dinosaur with no eyes?**

A: *Do-ya-think-he-saw-us*

**Q: Why did the ice cream cone become a reporter?**

A: *He wanted to get the scoop.*

**Q: What is green and can sing?**

A: *Elvis parsley*

**Q: What did the peanut butter say to the bread?**

A: *Quit loafing around.*

**Q: Why was the sewing machine so funny?**

A: *It kept everyone in stitches.*

**Q: Why did the hotdog turn down the chance to be in the movies?**

A: *because none of the roles were good enough.*

**Q: What did the cookie say when he wasn't feeling well?**

*A: I feel really crummy.*

**Q: Why did the lady throw butter out of the window?**

*A: She wanted to see a butter-fly.*

**Q: Why was the broom late for school?**

*A: It over-swept.*

**Q: What do you sing at a snowman's birthday party?**

*A: Freeze a jolly good fellow*

**Q: What's the difference between broccoli and bogey's?**

*A: Kids won't eat broccoli.*

**Q. What does a monster eat after he's had his teeth pulled?**

*A: The dentist*

**Q: What kind of snake is good at maths?**

*A: An adder.*

**Q: Why aren't elephants allowed on beaches?**

*A: They can't keep their trunks up*

**Q: What do you call a gorilla wearing ear-muffs?**

*A: Anything you like! He can't hear you*

**Q: Why was the baby strawberry crying?**

*A: Because his mom and dad were in a jam.*

**Q: Why wouldn't the shrimp share his treasure?**

*A: Because he was a little shellfish*

**Q: What did the policeman say to his belly button?**

*A: You're under a vest*

**Q: What do you call a fake noodle?**

*A: An impasta*

**Q: Why shouldn't you write with a broken pencil?**

*A: Because it's pointless.*

**Q: What lies at the bottom of the ocean and twitches?**

*A: A nervous wreck*

**Q: What do you call a belt with a watch on it?**

*A: A waist of time*

**Q: What is the best day to go to the beach?**

*A: Sunday, of course*

**Q: Why did the birdie go to the hospital?**

*A: To get a tweetment*

**Q: Where did the computer go to dance?**

*A: To a disc-o*

**Q: Why is England the wettest country?**

*A: Because the queen has reigned there for years*

**Q: What happened to the dog that swallowed a firefly?**

*A: It barked with de-light*

**Q: What kind of bird sticks to sweaters?**

*A: a Vel-Crow*

**Q: Where do boats go when they get sick?**

*A: The dock*

**Q: What pet makes the loudest noise?**

*A: A trum-pet*

**Q: What do you call two fat people having a chat?**

*A: A heavy discussion*

**Q: What did the digital clock say to the grandfather clock?**

*A: Look grandpa, no hands.*

**Q: What is an astronaut's favorite place on a computer?**

*A: The Space bar.*

**Q: Which month do soldiers hate most?**

*A: The month of March.*

**Q: What is a cat's favorite color?**

*A: Purr-ple*

**Q: Why did the dinosaur cross the road?**

*A: Because the chicken joke wasn't invented yet.*

**Q: Why couldn't dracula's wife get to sleep?**

*A: Because of his coffin.*

**Q: What did the worker at the rubber band factory say when he lost his job?**

*A: Oh Snap.*

**Q: What did the lawyer name his daughter?**

*A. Sue*

**Q: Why is Peter Pan always flying?**

*A: He never lands*

**Q: Why did the picture go to jail?**

*A: Because it was framed*

**Q: What kind of key opens a banana?**

*A: A monkey*

**Q: What do you call a guy who never farts in public?**

*A: A private tutor*

**Q: What did the horse say when he fell?**

*A: Help, I've fallen and I can't giddy up*

**Q: What do you get if you cross a witch and an iceberg?**

*A: A cold spell*

**Q: What did the duck say to the bartender?**

A: *Put it on my bill*


**Q: How does a squid go into battle?**

A: *Well Armed*


**Q: Did the disappointed smoker get everything he wanted for Christmas?**

A: *Clothes, but no cigar.*


**Q: What do you call the heavy breathing someone makes while trying to hold a yoga pose?**

A: *Yoga pants.*


**Q: What do you call two witches who share a broom sticks?**

A: *Broom mates*


**Q: Where do cows hang their paintings?**

A: *In the mooo-seum.*


**Q: Why did the can crusher quit his job?**

A: *Because it was soda pressing.*


**Q: What do bees do if they want to use public transport?**

A: *Wait at a buzz stop*


**Q: What did the fashion police officer say to his sweater?**

A: *"Do you know why I pulled you over?"*

**Q: Why does a Moon-rock taste better than an Earth-rock?**

*A: Because it's a little meteor*

**Q: What did the buffalo say to his son when he left for college?**

*A: Bison*

**Q: Where do Volkswagens go when they get old?**

*A: The Old Volks home*

**Q: Why did the elephants get kicked out of the public pool?**

*A: They kept dropping their trunks.*

**Q: What's the most musical part of a chicken?**

*A: The drumstick*

**Q: What did the fisherman say to the magician?**

*A: Pick a cod, any cod*

**Q: Why couldn't the sesame seed leave the casino?**

*A: Because he was on a roll.*

**Q: How do snails fight?**

*A: They slug it out.*

**Q: Why do bananas wear suntan lotion?**

*A: Because they peel.*

**Q: Why are penguins socially awkward?**

*A: Because they can't break the ice.*

Q: Where do hamburgers go to dance?

A: *They go to the meat-ball*

Q: What kind of shoes do all spies wear?

A: *Sneakers*

Q: What did the penny say to the other penny?

A: *We make perfect cents.*

Q: How do you find a Princess?

A: *You follow the foot Prince.*

Q: Why do abcdefghijklmopqrstuvwxy & z hate hanging out with the letter n?

A: *Because n always has to be the center of attention.*

Q: What do you call someone who is afraid of Santa?

A: *A Clausterphobic*

Q: Why do gorillas have big nostrils?

A: *Because gorillas have big fingers.*

Q: What do you call a pony with a sore throat?

A: *A little horse*

Q: What's invisible and smells of Carrots?

A. *Rabbit farts*

Q: Who led ten thousand pigs up the hill and back down again?

A: *The grand old duke of pork.*

Q: Who shouted 'Knickers' at the big bad wolf?

A: *Little rude riding hood.*

Q: How did the sheep feel when little bo peep lost them?

A: *Baaaaaad really Baaaaaad.*

Q: What's the hardest thing about learning to ride a bike?

A: *The ground.*

Q: Why couldn't the biscuit find its way home?

A: *It had been wafer too long.*

Q: How do you know which end of a worm is its head?

A: *Tickle its tummy and see which end laughs.*

Q: What do you call a duck with a huge ice cream?

A: *A lucky ducky*

Q: what do you call the duck after he dropped in on his head?

A: *A mucky ducky*

Q: What makes more noise than a dinosaur?

A: *Two dinosaurs*

Q: What's covered in custard and always complains?

A: *Apple grumble*

**Q: Why didn't the teddy bear eat his lunch?**

A: Because he was stuffed

**Q: Why did the swordfish blush?**

A: Because the sea weed.

**Q: What do you get if you blow hot air down a rabbit hole?**

A: Hot cross bunnies.

**Q: What did one goldfish say to the other in there fish tank?**

A: Do you know how to drive this thing?

**Q: What do you call a girl with a frog on her head?**

A: Lilly.

**Q: What do you call a baby bear with no teeth?**

A: A gummy bear!

**Q: What is as big as an elephant but weighs nothing?**

A: Its shadow

**Q: What do you call a sleeping dinosaur?**

A: A dino-snore

**Q: There were 10 cats in a boat and one jumped out. How many were left?**

A: None, because they were copycats!

**Q: What do whales eat?**

A: Fish and ships.

**Q: What did the farmer call the cow that would not give him any milk?**

A: An udder failure.

**Q: What do you get from a bad-tempered shark?**

A: As far away as possible.

**Q: What fish only swims at night?**

A: A starfish.

**Q: Why did the elephant leave the circus?**

A: He was tired of working for peanuts.

**Q: What do you get when you cross a roll of wool and a kangaroo?**

A: A woolen jumper!

**Q: Why was the mouse afraid of the water?**

A: Catfish

**Q: How many skunks does it take to make a big stink?**

A: A phew.

**Q: What is a shark's favorite sandwich?**

A: Peanut butter and jellyfish.

**Q: What kind of dog always runs a fever?**

A: A hot dog!

**Q: What do you call a dog that likes bubble baths?**

A: A shampoodle.

**Q: Why does a giraffe have such a long neck?**

A: Because his feet stink

**Q: What goes: now you see me, now you don't, now you see me, now you don't?**

A: A snowman on a zebra crossing

**Q: What's a frog's favorite drink?**

A: Croak-a-cola.

**Q: What's an alligator's favorite drink?**

A: Gator-Ade.

**Q: What do you call snake with no clothes on?**

A: Snaked.

**Q: What do you call a dinosaur that never gives up?**

A: A try and try and try-ceratops.

**Q: What's a puppy's favorite kind of pizza?**

A: Pupperoni.

**Q: How does a hedgehog play leap-frog?**

*Very carefully.*

**Q: What do you give an elephant that's going to be sick?**

*Plenty of space.*

Made in the USA
Lexington, KY
16 August 2016